THIS BOOK BELONGS TO

EMAIL:

ADDRESS:

CONTACT:

PHONE:

START DATE	END DATE

MO   TU   WE   TH   FR   SA   SU
☐   ☐   ☐   ☐   ☐   ☐   ☐

DATE: /   /

PROJECT:

FOREMAN:

WEATHER

F° ____   C° ____   ____ AM   ____ PM

| HOURS DUE TO BAD WEATHER | ISSUED AND DELAYS |

NOTE: ____________________________________

COMPLETION DATE	DAYS AHEAD OF SCHEDULE	DAYS BEHIND SCHEDULE

SAFETY AND INCIDENTS

SAFETY ISSUES THAT NEED TO BE ADDRESSED	ACCIDENTS / INCIDENTS / STEPS NEEDED TO RESOLVE

SUMMARY OF THE WORK DONE TODAY

IMPORTANT NOTES

NAME	SIGNATURE

TODAY LABOR

INITIALS	TRADE	START	FINISH	PAID HOURS	OVERTIME	COMPANY
☐ EMPLOYEE ☐ CONTRUCTOR		AM	PM			
☐ EMPLOYEE ☐ CONTRUCTOR		AM	PM			
☐ EMPLOYEE ☐ CONTRUCTOR		AM	PM			
☐ EMPLOYEE ☐ CONTRUCTOR		AM	PM			
☐ EMPLOYEE ☐ CONTRUCTOR		AM	PM			
☐ EMPLOYEE ☐ CONTRUCTOR		AM	PM			
☐ EMPLOYEE ☐ CONTRUCTOR		AM	PM			
☐ EMPLOYEE ☐ CONTRUCTOR		AM	PM			

EQUIPMENT ON SITE	NO. OF UNITE	WORKING YES / NO

HIRED EQUIPMENT	NO. OF UNITE	EQUIPMENT RENTED	FROM	RATE

NAME: _______________________   SIGNATURE: _______________________

MO TU WE TH FR SA SU
☐   ☐   ☐   ☐   ☐   ☐   ☐

DATE: ___ / ___ / ___

PROJECT:

FOREMAN:

WEATHER

F° ____   C° ____   ____ AM   ____ PM

HOURS DUE TO BAD WEATHER

ISSUED AND DELAYS

NOTE: ________________________________

COMPLETION DATE	DAYS AHEAD OF SCHEDULE	DAYS BEHIND SCHEDULE

SAFETY AND INCIDENTS

SAFETY ISSUES THAT NEED TO BE ADDRESSED	ACCIDENTS / INCIDENTS / STEPS NEEDED TO RESOLVE

SUMMARY OF THE WORK DONE TODAY

IMPORTANT NOTES

NAME	SIGNATURE

TODAY LABOR

INITIALS	TRADE	START	FINISH	PAID HOURS	OVERTIME	COMPANY
☐ EMPLOYEE ☐ CONTRUCTOR		AM	PM			
☐ EMPLOYEE ☐ CONTRUCTOR		AM	PM			
☐ EMPLOYEE ☐ CONTRUCTOR		AM	PM			
☐ EMPLOYEE ☐ CONTRUCTOR		AM	PM			
☐ EMPLOYEE ☐ CONTRUCTOR		AM	PM			
☐ EMPLOYEE ☐ CONTRUCTOR		AM	PM			
☐ EMPLOYEE ☐ CONTRUCTOR		AM	PM			
☐ EMPLOYEE ☐ CONTRUCTOR		AM	PM			

EQUIPMENT ON SITE	NO. OF UNITE	WORKING YES / NO

HIRED EQUIPMENT	NO. OF UNITE	EQUIPMENT RENTED	FROM	RATE

NAME: ______________________   SIGNATURE: ______________________

MO   TU   WE   TH   FR   SA   SU
☐   ☐   ☐   ☐   ☐   ☐   ☐

DATE: ___/___/___

PROJECT:

FOREMAN:

WEATHER

F° ______   C° ______   ______ AM   ______ PM

HOURS DUE TO BAD WEATHER

ISSUED AND DELAYS

NOTE: _______________________________________

COMPLETION DATE	DAYS AHEAD OF SCHEDULE	DAYS BEHIND SCHEDULE

SAFETY AND INCIDENTS

SAFETY ISSUES THAT NEED TO BE ADDRESSED	ACCIDENTS / INCIDENTS / STEPS NEEDED TO RESOLVE

SUMMARY OF THE WORK DONE TODAY

IMPORTANT NOTES

NAME	SIGNATURE

TODAY LABOR

INITIALS	TRADE	START	FINISH	PAID HOURS	OVERTIME	COMPANY
☐ EMPLOYEE ☐ CONTRUCTOR		AM	PM			
☐ EMPLOYEE ☐ CONTRUCTOR		AM	PM			
☐ EMPLOYEE ☐ CONTRUCTOR		AM	PM			
☐ EMPLOYEE ☐ CONTRUCTOR		AM	PM			
☐ EMPLOYEE ☐ CONTRUCTOR		AM	PM			
☐ EMPLOYEE ☐ CONTRUCTOR		AM	PM			
☐ EMPLOYEE ☐ CONTRUCTOR		AM	PM			
☐ EMPLOYEE ☐ CONTRUCTOR		AM	PM			

EQUIPMENT ON SITE	NO. OF UNITE	WORKING YES / NO

HIRED EQUIPMENT	NO. OF UNITE	EQUIPMENT RENTED	FROM	RATE

NAME: _______________________   SIGNATURE: _______________________

MO TU WE TH FR SA SU
☐   ☐   ☐   ☐   ☐   ☐   ☐

DATE: /   /

PROJECT:

FOREMAN:

WEATHER

F°_____ C°_____   _____ AM _____ PM

HOURS DUE TO BAD WEATHER

ISSUED AND DELAYS

NOTE: ____

COMPLETION DATE	DAYS AHEAD OF SCHEDULE	DAYS BEHIND SCHEDULE

SAFETY AND INCIDENTS

SAFETY ISSUES THAT NEED TO BE ADDRESSED	ACCIDENTS / INCIDENTS / STEPS NEEDED TO RESOLVE

SUMMARY OF THE WORK DONE TODAY

IMPORTANT NOTES

NAME	SIGNATURE

TODAY LABOR

INITIALS	TRADE	START	FINISH	PAID HOURS	OVERTIME	COMPANY
☐ EMPLOYEE ☐ CONTRUCTOR		AM	PM			
☐ EMPLOYEE ☐ CONTRUCTOR		AM	PM			
☐ EMPLOYEE ☐ CONTRUCTOR		AM	PM			
☐ EMPLOYEE ☐ CONTRUCTOR		AM	PM			
☐ EMPLOYEE ☐ CONTRUCTOR		AM	PM			
☐ EMPLOYEE ☐ CONTRUCTOR		AM	PM			
☐ EMPLOYEE ☐ CONTRUCTOR		AM	PM			
☐ EMPLOYEE ☐ CONTRUCTOR		AM	PM			

EQUIPMENT ON SITE	NO. OF UNITE	WORKING YES / NO

HIRED EQUIPMENT	NO. OF UNITE	EQUIPMENT RENTED	FROM	RATE

NAME: _______________________   SIGNATURE: _______________________

MO   TU   WE   TH   FR   SA   SU
☐   ☐   ☐   ☐   ☐   ☐   ☐

DATE: /   /

PROJECT:

FOREMAN:

WEATHER

F°_____ C°_____   _____ AM   _____ PM

HOURS DUE TO BAD WEATHER

ISSUED AND DELAYS

NOTE: ___________________________________

COMPLETION DATE	DAYS AHEAD OF SCHEDULE	DAYS BEHIND SCHEDULE

SAFETY AND INCIDENTS

SAFETY ISSUES THAT NEED TO BE ADDRESSED	ACCIDENTS / INCIDENTS / STEPS NEEDED TO RESOLVE

SUMMARY OF THE WORK DONE TODAY

IMPORTANT NOTES

NAME	SIGNATURE

TODAY LABOR

INITIALS	TRADE	START	FINISH	PAID HOURS	OVERTIME	COMPANY
☐ EMPLOYEE ☐ CONTRUCTOR		AM	PM			
☐ EMPLOYEE ☐ CONTRUCTOR		AM	PM			
☐ EMPLOYEE ☐ CONTRUCTOR		AM	PM			
☐ EMPLOYEE ☐ CONTRUCTOR		AM	PM			
☐ EMPLOYEE ☐ CONTRUCTOR		AM	PM			
☐ EMPLOYEE ☐ CONTRUCTOR		AM	PM			
☐ EMPLOYEE ☐ CONTRUCTOR		AM	PM			
☐ EMPLOYEE ☐ CONTRUCTOR		AM	PM			

EQUIPMENT ON SITE	NO. OF UNITE	WORKING YES / NO

HIRED EQUIPMENT	NO. OF UNITE	EQUIPMENT RENTED	FROM	RATE

NAME: _______________________   SIGNATURE: _______________________

MO TU WE TH FR SA SU
☐   ☐   ☐   ☐   ☐   ☐   ☐

DATE: /   /

PROJECT:

FOREMAN:

WEATHER

F°_____ C°_____   _____ AM _____ PM

| HOURS DUE TO BAD WEATHER | ISSUED AND DELAYS |

NOTE: _______________________________________

| COMPLETION DATE | DAYS AHEAD OF SCHEDULE | DAYS BEHIND SCHEDULE |

SAFETY AND INCIDENTS

| SAFETY ISSUES THAT NEED TO BE ADDRESSED | ACCIDENTS / INCIDENTS / STEPS NEEDED TO RESOLVE |

SUMMARY OF THE WORK DONE TODAY

IMPORTANT NOTES

| NAME | SIGNATURE |

TODAY LABOR

INITIALS	TRADE	START	FINISH	PAID HOURS	OVERTIME	COMPANY
☐ EMPLOYEE ☐ CONTRUCTOR		AM	PM			
☐ EMPLOYEE ☐ CONTRUCTOR		AM	PM			
☐ EMPLOYEE ☐ CONTRUCTOR		AM	PM			
☐ EMPLOYEE ☐ CONTRUCTOR		AM	PM			
☐ EMPLOYEE ☐ CONTRUCTOR		AM	PM			
☐ EMPLOYEE ☐ CONTRUCTOR		AM	PM			
☐ EMPLOYEE ☐ CONTRUCTOR		AM	PM			
☐ EMPLOYEE ☐ CONTRUCTOR		AM	PM			

EQUIPMENT ON SITE	NO. OF UNITE	WORKING YES / NO

HIRED EQUIPMENT	NO. OF UNITE	EQUIPMENT RENTED	FROM	RATE

NAME: _______________________   SIGNATURE: _______________________

MO TU WE TH FR SA SU
☐   ☐   ☐   ☐   ☐   ☐   ☐

DATE: /   /

PROJECT:

FOREMAN:

WEATHER

F°____ C°____   ____ AM ____ PM

HOURS DUE TO BAD WEATHER

ISSUED AND DELAYS

NOTE: ____________________

COMPLETION DATE	DAYS AHEAD OF SCHEDULE	DAYS BEHIND SCHEDULE

SAFETY AND INCIDENTS

SAFETY ISSUES THAT NEED TO BE ADDRESSED	ACCIDENTS / INCIDENTS / STEPS NEEDED TO RESOLVE

SUMMARY OF THE WORK DONE TODAY

IMPORTANT NOTES

NAME	SIGNATURE

TODAY LABOR

INITIALS	TRADE	START	FINISH	PAID HOURS	OVERTIME	COMPANY
☐ EMPLOYEE ☐ CONTRUCTOR		AM	PM			
☐ EMPLOYEE ☐ CONTRUCTOR		AM	PM			
☐ EMPLOYEE ☐ CONTRUCTOR		AM	PM			
☐ EMPLOYEE ☐ CONTRUCTOR		AM	PM			
☐ EMPLOYEE ☐ CONTRUCTOR		AM	PM			
☐ EMPLOYEE ☐ CONTRUCTOR		AM	PM			
☐ EMPLOYEE ☐ CONTRUCTOR		AM	PM			
☐ EMPLOYEE ☐ CONTRUCTOR		AM	PM			

EQUIPMENT ON SITE	NO. OF UNITE	WORKING YES / NO

HIRED EQUIPMENT	NO. OF UNITE	EQUIPMENT RENTED	FROM	RATE

NAME: _______________________   SIGNATURE: _______________________

MO TU WE TH FR SA SU
☐   ☐   ☐   ☐   ☐   ☐   ☐

DATE: /   /

PROJECT:

FOREMAN:

WEATHER

F°_____ C°_____   _____ AM   _____ PM

HOURS DUE TO BAD WEATHER	ISSUED AND DELAYS

NOTE: ____

COMPLETION DATE	DAYS AHEAD OF SCHEDULE	DAYS BEHIND SCHEDULE

SAFETY AND INCIDENTS

SAFETY ISSUES THAT NEED TO BE ADDRESSED	ACCIDENTS / INCIDENTS / STEPS NEEDED TO RESOLVE

SUMMARY OF THE WORK DONE TODAY

IMPORTANT NOTES

NAME	SIGNATURE

TODAY LABOR

INITIALS	TRADE	START	FINISH	PAID HOURS	OVERTIME	COMPANY
☐ EMPLOYEE ☐ CONTRUCTOR		AM	PM			
☐ EMPLOYEE ☐ CONTRUCTOR		AM	PM			
☐ EMPLOYEE ☐ CONTRUCTOR		AM	PM			
☐ EMPLOYEE ☐ CONTRUCTOR		AM	PM			
☐ EMPLOYEE ☐ CONTRUCTOR		AM	PM			
☐ EMPLOYEE ☐ CONTRUCTOR		AM	PM			
☐ EMPLOYEE ☐ CONTRUCTOR		AM	PM			
☐ EMPLOYEE ☐ CONTRUCTOR		AM	PM			

EQUIPMENT ON SITE	NO. OF UNITE	WORKING YES / NO

HIRED EQUIPMENT	NO. OF UNITE	EQUIPMENT RENTED	FROM	RATE

NAME: _______________________ SIGNATURE: _______________________

MO   TU   WE   TH   FR   SA   SU
☐   ☐   ☐   ☐   ☐   ☐   ☐

DATE: ___ / ___ / ___

PROJECT:

FOREMAN:

WEATHER

F° _____   C° _____   _____ AM   _____ PM

HOURS DUE TO BAD WEATHER

ISSUED AND DELAYS

NOTE: ____

COMPLETION DATE	DAYS AHEAD OF SCHEDULE	DAYS BEHIND SCHEDULE

SAFETY AND INCIDENTS

SAFETY ISSUES THAT NEED TO BE ADDRESSED	ACCIDENTS / INCIDENTS / STEPS NEEDED TO RESOLVE

SUMMARY OF THE WORK DONE TODAY

IMPORTANT NOTES

NAME	SIGNATURE

TODAY LABOR

INITIALS	TRADE	START	FINISH	PAID HOURS	OVERTIME	COMPANY
☐ EMPLOYEE ☐ CONTRUCTOR		AM	PM			
☐ EMPLOYEE ☐ CONTRUCTOR		AM	PM			
☐ EMPLOYEE ☐ CONTRUCTOR		AM	PM			
☐ EMPLOYEE ☐ CONTRUCTOR		AM	PM			
☐ EMPLOYEE ☐ CONTRUCTOR		AM	PM			
☐ EMPLOYEE ☐ CONTRUCTOR		AM	PM			
☐ EMPLOYEE ☐ CONTRUCTOR		AM	PM			
☐ EMPLOYEE ☐ CONTRUCTOR		AM	PM			

EQUIPMENT ON SITE	NO. OF UNITE	WORKING YES / NO

HIRED EQUIPMENT	NO. OF UNITE	EQUIPMENT RENTED	FROM	RATE

NAME: _______________________   SIGNATURE: _______________________

MO TU WE TH FR SA SU
☐   ☐   ☐   ☐   ☐   ☐   ☐

DATE: /   /

PROJECT:

FOREMAN:

WEATHER

F° _____ C° _____   _____ AM _____ PM

| HOURS DUE TO BAD WEATHER | ISSUED AND DELAYS |

NOTE: ____

COMPLETION DATE	DAYS AHEAD OF SCHEDULE	DAYS BEHIND SCHEDULE

SAFETY AND INCIDENTS

SAFETY ISSUES THAT NEED TO BE ADDRESSED	ACCIDENTS / INCIDENTS / STEPS NEEDED TO RESOLVE

SUMMARY OF THE WORK DONE TODAY

IMPORTANT NOTES

NAME	SIGNATURE

TODAY LABOR

INITIALS	TRADE	START	FINISH	PAID HOURS	OVERTIME	COMPANY
☐ EMPLOYEE ☐ CONTRUCTOR		AM	PM			
☐ EMPLOYEE ☐ CONTRUCTOR		AM	PM			
☐ EMPLOYEE ☐ CONTRUCTOR		AM	PM			
☐ EMPLOYEE ☐ CONTRUCTOR		AM	PM			
☐ EMPLOYEE ☐ CONTRUCTOR		AM	PM			
☐ EMPLOYEE ☐ CONTRUCTOR		AM	PM			
☐ EMPLOYEE ☐ CONTRUCTOR		AM	PM			
☐ EMPLOYEE ☐ CONTRUCTOR		AM	PM			

EQUIPMENT ON SITE	NO. OF UNITE	WORKING YES / NO

HIRED EQUIPMENT	NO. OF UNITE	EQUIPMENT RENTED	FROM	RATE

NAME: _______________________   SIGNATURE: _______________________

MO   TU   WE   TH   FR   SA   SU
☐   ☐   ☐   ☐   ☐   ☐   ☐

DATE: /   /

PROJECT:

FOREMAN:

WEATHER   F° ____   C° ____   ____ AM   ____ PM

HOURS DUE TO
BAD WEATHER

ISSUED AND DELAYS

NOTE: ____

COMPLETION DATE	DAYS AHEAD OF SCHEDULE	DAYS BEHIND SCHEDULE

SAFETY AND INCIDENTS

SAFETY ISSUES THAT NEED TO BE ADDRESSED	ACCIDENTS / INCIDENTS / STEPS NEEDED TO RESOLVE

SUMMARY OF THE WORK DONE TODAY

IMPORTANT NOTES

NAME	SIGNATURE

TODAY LABOR

INITIALS	TRADE	START	FINISH	PAID HOURS	OVERTIME	COMPANY
☐ EMPLOYEE ☐ CONTRUCTOR		AM	PM			
☐ EMPLOYEE ☐ CONTRUCTOR		AM	PM			
☐ EMPLOYEE ☐ CONTRUCTOR		AM	PM			
☐ EMPLOYEE ☐ CONTRUCTOR		AM	PM			
☐ EMPLOYEE ☐ CONTRUCTOR		AM	PM			
☐ EMPLOYEE ☐ CONTRUCTOR		AM	PM			
☐ EMPLOYEE ☐ CONTRUCTOR		AM	PM			
☐ EMPLOYEE ☐ CONTRUCTOR		AM	PM			

EQUIPMENT ON SITE	NO. OF UNITE	WORKING YES / NO

HIRED EQUIPMENT	NO. OF UNITE	EQUIPMENT RENTED	FROM	RATE

NAME: _______________________ SIGNATURE: _______________________

MO TU WE TH FR SA SU
☐   ☐   ☐   ☐   ☐   ☐   ☐

DATE: /   /

PROJECT:

FOREMAN:

WEATHER

F°_____ C°_____   _____ AM _____ PM

HOURS DUE TO BAD WEATHER

ISSUED AND DELAYS

NOTE: ____

COMPLETION DATE	DAYS AHEAD OF SCHEDULE	DAYS BEHIND SCHEDULE

SAFETY AND INCIDENTS

SAFETY ISSUES THAT NEED TO BE ADDRESSED	ACCIDENTS / INCIDENTS / STEPS NEEDED TO RESOLVE

SUMMARY OF THE WORK DONE TODAY

IMPORTANT NOTES

NAME	SIGNATURE

TODAY LABOR

INITIALS	TRADE	START	FINISH	PAID HOURS	OVERTIME	COMPANY
☐ EMPLOYEE ☐ CONTRUCTOR		AM	PM			
☐ EMPLOYEE ☐ CONTRUCTOR		AM	PM			
☐ EMPLOYEE ☐ CONTRUCTOR		AM	PM			
☐ EMPLOYEE ☐ CONTRUCTOR		AM	PM			
☐ EMPLOYEE ☐ CONTRUCTOR		AM	PM			
☐ EMPLOYEE ☐ CONTRUCTOR		AM	PM			
☐ EMPLOYEE ☐ CONTRUCTOR		AM	PM			
☐ EMPLOYEE ☐ CONTRUCTOR		AM	PM			

EQUIPMENT ON SITE	NO. OF UNITE	WORKING YES / NO

HIRED EQUIPMENT	NO. OF UNITE	EQUIPMENT RENTED	FROM	RATE

NAME: _______________________ SIGNATURE: _______________________

MO   TU   WE   TH   FR   SA   SU
☐   ☐   ☐   ☐   ☐   ☐   ☐

DATE: ___ / ___ / ___

PROJECT:

FOREMAN:

WEATHER

F° _______   C° _______   _______ AM   _______ PM

HOURS DUE TO BAD WEATHER

ISSUED AND DELAYS

NOTE: ____

COMPLETION DATE	DAYS AHEAD OF SCHEDULE	DAYS BEHIND SCHEDULE

SAFETY AND INCIDENTS

SAFETY ISSUES THAT NEED TO BE ADDRESSED	ACCIDENTS / INCIDENTS / STEPS NEEDED TO RESOLVE

SUMMARY OF THE WORK DONE TODAY

IMPORTANT NOTES

NAME	SIGNATURE

TODAY LABOR

INITIALS	TRADE	START	FINISH	PAID HOURS	OVERTIME	COMPANY
☐ EMPLOYEE ☐ CONTRUCTOR		AM	PM			
☐ EMPLOYEE ☐ CONTRUCTOR		AM	PM			
☐ EMPLOYEE ☐ CONTRUCTOR		AM	PM			
☐ EMPLOYEE ☐ CONTRUCTOR		AM	PM			
☐ EMPLOYEE ☐ CONTRUCTOR		AM	PM			
☐ EMPLOYEE ☐ CONTRUCTOR		AM	PM			
☐ EMPLOYEE ☐ CONTRUCTOR		AM	PM			
☐ EMPLOYEE ☐ CONTRUCTOR		AM	PM			

EQUIPMENT ON SITE	NO. OF UNITE	WORKING YES / NO

HIRED EQUIPMENT	NO. OF UNITE	EQUIPMENT RENTED	FROM	RATE

NAME: _______________________   SIGNATURE: _______________________

MO   TU   WE   TH   FR   SA   SU
☐   ☐   ☐   ☐   ☐   ☐   ☐

DATE: ___/___/___

PROJECT:

FOREMAN:

WEATHER

F° ______ C° ______ ______ AM ______ PM

HOURS DUE TO BAD WEATHER

ISSUED AND DELAYS

NOTE: ____

COMPLETION DATE	DAYS AHEAD OF SCHEDULE	DAYS BEHIND SCHEDULE

SAFETY AND INCIDENTS

SAFETY ISSUES THAT NEED TO BE ADDRESSED	ACCIDENTS / INCIDENTS / STEPS NEEDED TO RESOLVE

SUMMARY OF THE WORK DONE TODAY

IMPORTANT NOTES

NAME	SIGNATURE

TODAY LABOR

INITIALS	TRADE	START	FINISH	PAID HOURS	OVERTIME	COMPANY
☐ EMPLOYEE ☐ CONTRUCTOR		AM	PM			
☐ EMPLOYEE ☐ CONTRUCTOR		AM	PM			
☐ EMPLOYEE ☐ CONTRUCTOR		AM	PM			
☐ EMPLOYEE ☐ CONTRUCTOR		AM	PM			
☐ EMPLOYEE ☐ CONTRUCTOR		AM	PM			
☐ EMPLOYEE ☐ CONTRUCTOR		AM	PM			
☐ EMPLOYEE ☐ CONTRUCTOR		AM	PM			
☐ EMPLOYEE ☐ CONTRUCTOR		AM	PM			

EQUIPMENT ON SITE	NO. OF UNITE	WORKING YES / NO

HIRED EQUIPMENT	NO. OF UNITE	EQUIPMENT RENTED	FROM	RATE

NAME: _______________________ SIGNATURE: _______________________

MO   TU   WE   TH   FR   SA   SU   **DATE:**   /   /

☐   ☐   ☐   ☐   ☐   ☐   ☐

PROJECT: **FOREMAN:**

WEATHER   F° _____   C° _____   _____ AM   _____ PM

HOURS DUE TO BAD WEATHER	ISSUED AND DELAYS

NOTE: _______________________________________

COMPLETION DATE	DAYS AHEAD OF SCHEDULE	DAYS BEHIND SCHEDULE

SAFETY AND INCIDENTS

SAFETY ISSUES THAT NEED TO BE ADDRESSED	ACCIDENTS / INCIDENTS / STEPS NEEDED TO RESOLVE

SUMMARY OF THE WORK DONE TODAY

IMPORTANT NOTES

NAME	SIGNATURE

TODAY LABOR

INITIALS	TRADE	START	FINISH	PAID HOURS	OVERTIME	COMPANY
☐ EMPLOYEE ☐ CONTRUCTOR		AM	PM			
☐ EMPLOYEE ☐ CONTRUCTOR		AM	PM			
☐ EMPLOYEE ☐ CONTRUCTOR		AM	PM			
☐ EMPLOYEE ☐ CONTRUCTOR		AM	PM			
☐ EMPLOYEE ☐ CONTRUCTOR		AM	PM			
☐ EMPLOYEE ☐ CONTRUCTOR		AM	PM			
☐ EMPLOYEE ☐ CONTRUCTOR		AM	PM			
☐ EMPLOYEE ☐ CONTRUCTOR		AM	PM			

EQUIPMENT ON SITE	NO. OF UNITE	WORKING YES / NO

HIRED EQUIPMENT	NO. OF UNITE	EQUIPMENT RENTED	FROM	RATE

NAME: _______________________   SIGNATURE: _______________________

MO TU WE TH FR SA SU
☐   ☐   ☐   ☐   ☐   ☐   ☐

DATE: /   /

PROJECT:

FOREMAN:

WEATHER

F° _____ C° _____   _____ AM _____ PM

| HOURS DUE TO BAD WEATHER | ISSUED AND DELAYS |

NOTE: ____

COMPLETION DATE	DAYS AHEAD OF SCHEDULE	DAYS BEHIND SCHEDULE

SAFETY AND INCIDENTS

SAFETY ISSUES THAT NEED TO BE ADDRESSED	ACCIDENTS / INCIDENTS / STEPS NEEDED TO RESOLVE

SUMMARY OF THE WORK DONE TODAY

IMPORTANT NOTES

NAME	SIGNATURE

TODAY LABOR

INITIALS	TRADE	START	FINISH	PAID HOURS	OVERTIME	COMPANY
☐ EMPLOYEE ☐ CONTRUCTOR		AM	PM			
☐ EMPLOYEE ☐ CONTRUCTOR		AM	PM			
☐ EMPLOYEE ☐ CONTRUCTOR		AM	PM			
☐ EMPLOYEE ☐ CONTRUCTOR		AM	PM			
☐ EMPLOYEE ☐ CONTRUCTOR		AM	PM			
☐ EMPLOYEE ☐ CONTRUCTOR		AM	PM			
☐ EMPLOYEE ☐ CONTRUCTOR		AM	PM			
☐ EMPLOYEE ☐ CONTRUCTOR		AM	PM			

EQUIPMENT ON SITE	NO. OF UNITE	WORKING YES / NO

HIRED EQUIPMENT	NO. OF UNITE	EQUIPMENT RENTED	FROM	RATE

NAME: _______________________   SIGNATURE: _______________________

MO TU WE TH FR SA SU
☐   ☐   ☐   ☐   ☐   ☐   ☐

DATE: ____ / ____ / ____

PROJECT:

FOREMAN:

WEATHER

F° ____ C° ____   ____ AM ____ PM

HOURS DUE TO BAD WEATHER	ISSUED AND DELAYS

NOTE: ____

COMPLETION DATE	DAYS AHEAD OF SCHEDULE	DAYS BEHIND SCHEDULE

SAFETY AND INCIDENTS

SAFETY ISSUES THAT NEED TO BE ADDRESSED	ACCIDENTS / INCIDENTS / STEPS NEEDED TO RESOLVE

SUMMARY OF THE WORK DONE TODAY

IMPORTANT NOTES

NAME	SIGNATURE

TODAY LABOR

INITIALS	TRADE	START	FINISH	PAID HOURS	OVERTIME	COMPANY
☐ EMPLOYEE ☐ CONTRUCTOR		AM	PM			
☐ EMPLOYEE ☐ CONTRUCTOR		AM	PM			
☐ EMPLOYEE ☐ CONTRUCTOR		AM	PM			
☐ EMPLOYEE ☐ CONTRUCTOR		AM	PM			
☐ EMPLOYEE ☐ CONTRUCTOR		AM	PM			
☐ EMPLOYEE ☐ CONTRUCTOR		AM	PM			
☐ EMPLOYEE ☐ CONTRUCTOR		AM	PM			
☐ EMPLOYEE ☐ CONTRUCTOR		AM	PM			

EQUIPMENT ON SITE	NO. OF UNITE	WORKING YES / NO

HIRED EQUIPMENT	NO. OF UNITE	EQUIPMENT RENTED	FROM	RATE

NAME: ______________________________   SIGNATURE: ______________________________

MO	TU	WE	TH	FR	SA	SU
☐	☐	☐	☐	☐	☐	☐

DATE: /   /

PROJECT:

FOREMAN:

WEATHER

F° _______ C° _______   _______ AM _______ PM

HOURS DUE TO BAD WEATHER

ISSUED AND DELAYS

NOTE: ____

COMPLETION DATE	DAYS AHEAD OF SCHEDULE	DAYS BEHIND SCHEDULE

SAFETY AND INCIDENTS

SAFETY ISSUES THAT NEED TO BE ADDRESSED	ACCIDENTS / INCIDENTS / STEPS NEEDED TO RESOLVE

SUMMARY OF THE WORK DONE TODAY

IMPORTANT NOTES

NAME	SIGNATURE

TODAY LABOR							
INITIALS	TRADE	START	FINISH		PAID HOURS	OVERTIME	COMPANY
☐ EMPLOYEE ☐ CONTRUCTOR		AM	PM				
☐ EMPLOYEE ☐ CONTRUCTOR		AM	PM				
☐ EMPLOYEE ☐ CONTRUCTOR		AM	PM				
☐ EMPLOYEE ☐ CONTRUCTOR		AM	PM				
☐ EMPLOYEE ☐ CONTRUCTOR		AM	PM				
☐ EMPLOYEE ☐ CONTRUCTOR		AM	PM				
☐ EMPLOYEE ☐ CONTRUCTOR		AM	PM				
☐ EMPLOYEE ☐ CONTRUCTOR		AM	PM				

EQUIPMENT ON SITE	NO. OF UNITE	WORKING YES / NO

HIRED EQUIPMENT	NO. OF UNITE	EQUIPMENT RENTED	FROM	RATE

NAME: _______________________   SIGNATURE: _______________________

MO   TU   WE   TH   FR   SA   SU
☐   ☐   ☐   ☐   ☐   ☐   ☐

DATE: ___/___/___

PROJECT:

FOREMAN:

WEATHER   F° _____ C° _____   _____ AM   _____ PM

HOURS DUE TO BAD WEATHER

ISSUED AND DELAYS

NOTE: _______________________

COMPLETION DATE	DAYS AHEAD OF SCHEDULE	DAYS BEHIND SCHEDULE

SAFETY AND INCIDENTS

SAFETY ISSUES THAT NEED TO BE ADDRESSED	ACCIDENTS / INCIDENTS / STEPS NEEDED TO RESOLVE

SUMMARY OF THE WORK DONE TODAY

IMPORTANT NOTES

NAME	SIGNATURE

TODAY LABOR

INITIALS	TRADE	START	FINISH	PAID HOURS	OVERTIME	COMPANY
☐ EMPLOYEE ☐ CONTRUCTOR		AM	PM			
☐ EMPLOYEE ☐ CONTRUCTOR		AM	PM			
☐ EMPLOYEE ☐ CONTRUCTOR		AM	PM			
☐ EMPLOYEE ☐ CONTRUCTOR		AM	PM			
☐ EMPLOYEE ☐ CONTRUCTOR		AM	PM			
☐ EMPLOYEE ☐ CONTRUCTOR		AM	PM			
☐ EMPLOYEE ☐ CONTRUCTOR		AM	PM			
☐ EMPLOYEE ☐ CONTRUCTOR		AM	PM			

EQUIPMENT ON SITE	NO. OF UNITE	WORKING YES / NO

HIRED EQUIPMENT	NO. OF UNITE	EQUIPMENT RENTED	FROM	RATE

NAME: _______________________________   SIGNATURE: _______________________________

MO TU WE TH FR SA SU
☐   ☐   ☐   ☐   ☐   ☐   ☐

DATE: __/__/__

PROJECT:

FOREMAN:

WEATHER

F°____ C°____ ____AM ____PM

HOURS DUE TO BAD WEATHER

ISSUED AND DELAYS

NOTE: ____

COMPLETION DATE	DAYS AHEAD OF SCHEDULE	DAYS BEHIND SCHEDULE

SAFETY AND INCIDENTS

SAFETY ISSUES THAT NEED TO BE ADDRESSED	ACCIDENTS / INCIDENTS / STEPS NEEDED TO RESOLVE

SUMMARY OF THE WORK DONE TODAY

IMPORTANT NOTES

NAME	SIGNATURE

TODAY LABOR

INITIALS	TRADE	START	FINISH	PAID HOURS	OVERTIME	COMPANY
☐ EMPLOYEE ☐ CONTRUCTOR		AM	PM			
☐ EMPLOYEE ☐ CONTRUCTOR		AM	PM			
☐ EMPLOYEE ☐ CONTRUCTOR		AM	PM			
☐ EMPLOYEE ☐ CONTRUCTOR		AM	PM			
☐ EMPLOYEE ☐ CONTRUCTOR		AM	PM			
☐ EMPLOYEE ☐ CONTRUCTOR		AM	PM			
☐ EMPLOYEE ☐ CONTRUCTOR		AM	PM			
☐ EMPLOYEE ☐ CONTRUCTOR		AM	PM			

EQUIPMENT ON SITE	NO. OF UNITE	WORKING YES / NO

HIRED EQUIPMENT	NO. OF UNITE	EQUIPMENT RENTED	FROM	RATE

NAME: ___________________________   SIGNATURE: ___________________________

MO   TU   WE   TH   FR   SA   SU
☐   ☐   ☐   ☐   ☐   ☐   ☐   DATE: /   /

PROJECT: FOREMAN:

WEATHER   HOURS DUE TO   ISSUED AND DELAYS
         F°____ C°____   ____ AM ____ PM   BAD WEATHER

NOTE: ____

COMPLETION DATE	DAYS AHEAD OF SCHEDULE	DAYS BEHIND SCHEDULE

SAFETY AND INCIDENTS

SAFETY ISSUES THAT NEED TO BE ADDRESSED	ACCIDENTS / INCIDENTS / STEPS NEEDED TO RESOLVE

SUMMARY OF THE WORK DONE TODAY

IMPORTANT NOTES

NAME	SIGNATURE

TODAY LABOR

INITIALS	TRADE	START	FINISH	PAID HOURS	OVERTIME	COMPANY
☐ EMPLOYEE ☐ CONTRUCTOR		AM	PM			
☐ EMPLOYEE ☐ CONTRUCTOR		AM	PM			
☐ EMPLOYEE ☐ CONTRUCTOR		AM	PM			
☐ EMPLOYEE ☐ CONTRUCTOR		AM	PM			
☐ EMPLOYEE ☐ CONTRUCTOR		AM	PM			
☐ EMPLOYEE ☐ CONTRUCTOR		AM	PM			
☐ EMPLOYEE ☐ CONTRUCTOR		AM	PM			
☐ EMPLOYEE ☐ CONTRUCTOR		AM	PM			

EQUIPMENT ON SITE	NO. OF UNITE	WORKING YES / NO

HIRED EQUIPMENT	NO. OF UNITE	EQUIPMENT RENTED	FROM	RATE

NAME: _______________________   SIGNATURE: _______________________

MO TU WE TH FR SA SU
☐   ☐   ☐   ☐   ☐   ☐   ☐

DATE: /   /

PROJECT:

FOREMAN:

WEATHER   F°_____ C°_____   _____ AM _____ PM

HOURS DUE TO BAD WEATHER

ISSUED AND DELAYS

NOTE: ____

COMPLETION DATE	DAYS AHEAD OF SCHEDULE	DAYS BEHIND SCHEDULE

SAFETY AND INCIDENTS

SAFETY ISSUES THAT NEED TO BE ADDRESSED	ACCIDENTS / INCIDENTS / STEPS NEEDED TO RESOLVE

SUMMARY OF THE WORK DONE TODAY

IMPORTANT NOTES

NAME	SIGNATURE

TODAY LABOR

INITIALS	TRADE	START	FINISH	PAID HOURS	OVERTIME	COMPANY
☐ EMPLOYEE ☐ CONTRUCTOR		AM	PM			
☐ EMPLOYEE ☐ CONTRUCTOR		AM	PM			
☐ EMPLOYEE ☐ CONTRUCTOR		AM	PM			
☐ EMPLOYEE ☐ CONTRUCTOR		AM	PM			
☐ EMPLOYEE ☐ CONTRUCTOR		AM	PM			
☐ EMPLOYEE ☐ CONTRUCTOR		AM	PM			
☐ EMPLOYEE ☐ CONTRUCTOR		AM	PM			
☐ EMPLOYEE ☐ CONTRUCTOR		AM	PM			

EQUIPMENT ON SITE	NO. OF UNITE	WORKING YES / NO

HIRED EQUIPMENT	NO. OF UNITE	EQUIPMENT RENTED	FROM	RATE

NAME: _______________________________   SIGNATURE: _______________________________

MO   TU   WE   TH   FR   SA   SU
☐   ☐   ☐   ☐   ☐   ☐   ☐

DATE: /   /

PROJECT:

FOREMAN:

WEATHER

F°____   C°____   ____ AM   ____ PM

HOURS DUE TO
BAD WEATHER

ISSUED AND DELAYS

NOTE: ____

COMPLETION DATE	DAYS AHEAD OF SCHEDULE	DAYS BEHIND SCHEDULE

SAFETY AND INCIDENTS

SAFETY ISSUES THAT NEED TO BE ADDRESSED	ACCIDENTS / INCIDENTS / STEPS NEEDED TO RESOLVE

SUMMARY OF THE WORK DONE TODAY

IMPORTANT NOTES

NAME	SIGNATURE

TODAY LABOR

INITIALS	TRADE	START	FINISH	PAID HOURS	OVERTIME	COMPANY
☐ EMPLOYEE ☐ CONTRUCTOR		AM	PM			
☐ EMPLOYEE ☐ CONTRUCTOR		AM	PM			
☐ EMPLOYEE ☐ CONTRUCTOR		AM	PM			
☐ EMPLOYEE ☐ CONTRUCTOR		AM	PM			
☐ EMPLOYEE ☐ CONTRUCTOR		AM	PM			
☐ EMPLOYEE ☐ CONTRUCTOR		AM	PM			
☐ EMPLOYEE ☐ CONTRUCTOR		AM	PM			
☐ EMPLOYEE ☐ CONTRUCTOR		AM	PM			

EQUIPMENT ON SITE	NO. OF UNITE	WORKING YES / NO

HIRED EQUIPMENT	NO. OF UNITE	EQUIPMENT RENTED	FROM	RATE

NAME: _______________________   SIGNATURE: _______________________

MO TU WE TH FR SA SU
☐   ☐   ☐   ☐   ☐   ☐   ☐

DATE: /   /

PROJECT:

FOREMAN:

WEATHER

F°_____ C°_____   _____ AM _____ PM

HOURS DUE TO BAD WEATHER	ISSUED AND DELAYS

NOTE: ____

COMPLETION DATE	DAYS AHEAD OF SCHEDULE	DAYS BEHIND SCHEDULE

SAFETY AND INCIDENTS

SAFETY ISSUES THAT NEED TO BE ADDRESSED	ACCIDENTS / INCIDENTS / STEPS NEEDED TO RESOLVE

SUMMARY OF THE WORK DONE TODAY

IMPORTANT NOTES

NAME	SIGNATURE

<table>
<tr><td colspan="8" align="center">TODAY LABOR</td></tr>
<tr><td>INITIALS</td><td>TRADE</td><td>START</td><td>FINISH</td><td>PAID HOURS</td><td>OVERTIME</td><td>COMPANY</td></tr>
<tr><td>☐ EMPLOYEE
☐ CONTRUCTOR</td><td></td><td>AM</td><td>PM</td><td></td><td></td><td></td></tr>
<tr><td>☐ EMPLOYEE
☐ CONTRUCTOR</td><td></td><td>AM</td><td>PM</td><td></td><td></td><td></td></tr>
<tr><td>☐ EMPLOYEE
☐ CONTRUCTOR</td><td></td><td>AM</td><td>PM</td><td></td><td></td><td></td></tr>
<tr><td>☐ EMPLOYEE
☐ CONTRUCTOR</td><td></td><td>AM</td><td>PM</td><td></td><td></td><td></td></tr>
<tr><td>☐ EMPLOYEE
☐ CONTRUCTOR</td><td></td><td>AM</td><td>PM</td><td></td><td></td><td></td></tr>
<tr><td>☐ EMPLOYEE
☐ CONTRUCTOR</td><td></td><td>AM</td><td>PM</td><td></td><td></td><td></td></tr>
<tr><td>☐ EMPLOYEE
☐ CONTRUCTOR</td><td></td><td>AM</td><td>PM</td><td></td><td></td><td></td></tr>
<tr><td>☐ EMPLOYEE
☐ CONTRUCTOR</td><td></td><td>AM</td><td>PM</td><td></td><td></td><td></td></tr>
</table>

EQUIPMENT ON SITE	NO. OF UNITE	WORKING YES / NO

HIRED EQUIPMENT	NO. OF UNITE	EQUIPMENT RENTED	FROM	RATE

NAME: _______________________   SIGNATURE: _______________________

MO   TU   WE   TH   FR   SA   SU
☐   ☐   ☐   ☐   ☐   ☐   ☐

DATE: ___ / ___ / ___

PROJECT:

FOREMAN:

WEATHER   F° ___   C° ___   ___ AM   ___ PM

HOURS DUE TO BAD WEATHER

ISSUED AND DELAYS

NOTE: ____

COMPLETION DATE	DAYS AHEAD OF SCHEDULE	DAYS BEHIND SCHEDULE

SAFETY AND INCIDENTS

SAFETY ISSUES THAT NEED TO BE ADDRESSED	ACCIDENTS / INCIDENTS / STEPS NEEDED TO RESOLVE

SUMMARY OF THE WORK DONE TODAY

IMPORTANT NOTES

NAME	SIGNATURE

TODAY LABOR

INITIALS	TRADE	START	FINISH	PAID HOURS	OVERTIME	COMPANY
☐ EMPLOYEE ☐ CONTRUCTOR		AM	PM			
☐ EMPLOYEE ☐ CONTRUCTOR		AM	PM			
☐ EMPLOYEE ☐ CONTRUCTOR		AM	PM			
☐ EMPLOYEE ☐ CONTRUCTOR		AM	PM			
☐ EMPLOYEE ☐ CONTRUCTOR		AM	PM			
☐ EMPLOYEE ☐ CONTRUCTOR		AM	PM			
☐ EMPLOYEE ☐ CONTRUCTOR		AM	PM			
☐ EMPLOYEE ☐ CONTRUCTOR		AM	PM			

EQUIPMENT ON SITE	NO. OF UNITE	WORKING YES / NO

HIRED EQUIPMENT	NO. OF UNITE	EQUIPMENT RENTED	FROM	RATE

NAME: _______________________   SIGNATURE: _______________________

MO TU WE TH FR SA SU
☐   ☐   ☐   ☐   ☐   ☐   ☐

DATE: /   /

PROJECT:

FOREMAN:

WEATHER

F°_____ C°_____   _____AM _____PM

| HOURS DUE TO BAD WEATHER | ISSUED AND DELAYS |

NOTE: _______________________________________

COMPLETION DATE	DAYS AHEAD OF SCHEDULE	DAYS BEHIND SCHEDULE

SAFETY AND INCIDENTS

SAFETY ISSUES THAT NEED TO BE ADDRESSED	ACCIDENTS / INCIDENTS / STEPS NEEDED TO RESOLVE

SUMMARY OF THE WORK DONE TODAY

IMPORTANT NOTES

NAME	SIGNATURE

TODAY LABOR

INITIALS	TRADE	START	FINISH	PAID HOURS	OVERTIME	COMPANY
☐ EMPLOYEE ☐ CONTRUCTOR		AM	PM			
☐ EMPLOYEE ☐ CONTRUCTOR		AM	PM			
☐ EMPLOYEE ☐ CONTRUCTOR		AM	PM			
☐ EMPLOYEE ☐ CONTRUCTOR		AM	PM			
☐ EMPLOYEE ☐ CONTRUCTOR		AM	PM			
☐ EMPLOYEE ☐ CONTRUCTOR		AM	PM			
☐ EMPLOYEE ☐ CONTRUCTOR		AM	PM			
☐ EMPLOYEE ☐ CONTRUCTOR		AM	PM			

EQUIPMENT ON SITE	NO. OF UNITE	WORKING YES / NO

HIRED EQUIPMENT	NO. OF UNITE	EQUIPMENT RENTED	FROM	RATE

NAME: ________________________   SIGNATURE: ________________________

MO TU WE TH FR SA SU
☐   ☐   ☐   ☐   ☐   ☐   ☐

DATE: ___ / ___ / ___

PROJECT:

FOREMAN:

WEATHER   F° _____ C° _____   _____ AM   _____ PM

HOURS DUE TO BAD WEATHER

ISSUED AND DELAYS

NOTE: _______________________________________

COMPLETION DATE	DAYS AHEAD OF SCHEDULE	DAYS BEHIND SCHEDULE

SAFETY AND INCIDENTS

SAFETY ISSUES THAT NEED TO BE ADDRESSED	ACCIDENTS / INCIDENTS / STEPS NEEDED TO RESOLVE

SUMMARY OF THE WORK DONE TODAY

____
____
____
____
____

IMPORTANT NOTES

____
____
____
____
____

NAME	SIGNATURE

TODAY LABOR

INITIALS	TRADE	START	FINISH	PAID HOURS	OVERTIME	COMPANY
☐ EMPLOYEE ☐ CONTRUCTOR		AM	PM			
☐ EMPLOYEE ☐ CONTRUCTOR		AM	PM			
☐ EMPLOYEE ☐ CONTRUCTOR		AM	PM			
☐ EMPLOYEE ☐ CONTRUCTOR		AM	PM			
☐ EMPLOYEE ☐ CONTRUCTOR		AM	PM			
☐ EMPLOYEE ☐ CONTRUCTOR		AM	PM			
☐ EMPLOYEE ☐ CONTRUCTOR		AM	PM			
☐ EMPLOYEE ☐ CONTRUCTOR		AM	PM			

EQUIPMENT ON SITE	NO. OF UNITE	WORKING YES / NO

HIRED EQUIPMENT	NO. OF UNITE	EQUIPMENT RENTED	FROM	RATE

NAME: ________________________   SIGNATURE: ________________________

MO TU WE TH FR SA SU
☐   ☐   ☐   ☐   ☐   ☐   ☐

DATE: /   /

PROJECT:

FOREMAN:

WEATHER

F°_____ C°_____   _____ AM _____ PM

| HOURS DUE TO BAD WEATHER | ISSUED AND DELAYS |

NOTE: ____

COMPLETION DATE	DAYS AHEAD OF SCHEDULE	DAYS BEHIND SCHEDULE

SAFETY AND INCIDENTS

SAFETY ISSUES THAT NEED TO BE ADDRESSED	ACCIDENTS / INCIDENTS / STEPS NEEDED TO RESOLVE

SUMMARY OF THE WORK DONE TODAY

IMPORTANT NOTES

NAME	SIGNATURE

TODAY LABOR

INITIALS	TRADE	START	FINISH	PAID HOURS	OVERTIME	COMPANY
☐ EMPLOYEE ☐ CONTRUCTOR		AM	PM			
☐ EMPLOYEE ☐ CONTRUCTOR		AM	PM			
☐ EMPLOYEE ☐ CONTRUCTOR		AM	PM			
☐ EMPLOYEE ☐ CONTRUCTOR		AM	PM			
☐ EMPLOYEE ☐ CONTRUCTOR		AM	PM			
☐ EMPLOYEE ☐ CONTRUCTOR		AM	PM			
☐ EMPLOYEE ☐ CONTRUCTOR		AM	PM			
☐ EMPLOYEE ☐ CONTRUCTOR		AM	PM			

EQUIPMENT ON SITE	NO. OF UNITE	WORKING YES / NO

HIRED EQUIPMENT	NO. OF UNITE	EQUIPMENT RENTED	FROM	RATE

NAME: ______________________   SIGNATURE: ______________________

MO   TU   WE   TH   FR   SA   SU
☐   ☐   ☐   ☐   ☐   ☐   ☐

DATE: /   /

PROJECT:

FOREMAN:

WEATHER

F° _____   C° _____   _____ AM   _____ PM

| HOURS DUE TO BAD WEATHER | ISSUED AND DELAYS |

NOTE: ____

COMPLETION DATE	DAYS AHEAD OF SCHEDULE	DAYS BEHIND SCHEDULE

SAFETY AND INCIDENTS

SAFETY ISSUES THAT NEED TO BE ADDRESSED	ACCIDENTS / INCIDENTS / STEPS NEEDED TO RESOLVE

SUMMARY OF THE WORK DONE TODAY

IMPORTANT NOTES

NAME	SIGNATURE

TODAY LABOR

INITIALS	TRADE	START	FINISH	PAID HOURS	OVERTIME	COMPANY
☐ EMPLOYEE ☐ CONTRUCTOR		AM	PM			
☐ EMPLOYEE ☐ CONTRUCTOR		AM	PM			
☐ EMPLOYEE ☐ CONTRUCTOR		AM	PM			
☐ EMPLOYEE ☐ CONTRUCTOR		AM	PM			
☐ EMPLOYEE ☐ CONTRUCTOR		AM	PM			
☐ EMPLOYEE ☐ CONTRUCTOR		AM	PM			
☐ EMPLOYEE ☐ CONTRUCTOR		AM	PM			
☐ EMPLOYEE ☐ CONTRUCTOR		AM	PM			

EQUIPMENT ON SITE	NO. OF UNITE	WORKING YES / NO

HIRED EQUIPMENT	NO. OF UNITE	EQUIPMENT RENTED	FROM	RATE

NAME: _______________________   SIGNATURE: _______________________

MO TU WE TH FR SA SU
☐   ☐   ☐   ☐   ☐   ☐   ☐

DATE: ___/___/___

PROJECT:

FOREMAN:

WEATHER

F°_____ C°_____   _____ AM _____ PM

HOURS DUE TO BAD WEATHER	ISSUED AND DELAYS

NOTE: ____

COMPLETION DATE	DAYS AHEAD OF SCHEDULE	DAYS BEHIND SCHEDULE

SAFETY AND INCIDENTS

SAFETY ISSUES THAT NEED TO BE ADDRESSED	ACCIDENTS / INCIDENTS / STEPS NEEDED TO RESOLVE

SUMMARY OF THE WORK DONE TODAY

IMPORTANT NOTES

NAME	SIGNATURE

TODAY LABOR

INITIALS	TRADE	START	FINISH	PAID HOURS	OVERTIME	COMPANY
☐ EMPLOYEE ☐ CONTRUCTOR		AM	PM			
☐ EMPLOYEE ☐ CONTRUCTOR		AM	PM			
☐ EMPLOYEE ☐ CONTRUCTOR		AM	PM			
☐ EMPLOYEE ☐ CONTRUCTOR		AM	PM			
☐ EMPLOYEE ☐ CONTRUCTOR		AM	PM			
☐ EMPLOYEE ☐ CONTRUCTOR		AM	PM			
☐ EMPLOYEE ☐ CONTRUCTOR		AM	PM			
☐ EMPLOYEE ☐ CONTRUCTOR		AM	PM			

EQUIPMENT ON SITE	NO. OF UNITE	WORKING YES / NO

HIRED EQUIPMENT	NO. OF UNITE	EQUIPMENT RENTED	FROM	RATE

NAME: _______________________   SIGNATURE: _______________________

MO TU WE TH FR SA SU
☐   ☐   ☐   ☐   ☐   ☐   ☐

DATE: /   /

PROJECT:

FOREMAN:

WEATHER   F°_____ C°_____   _____ AM _____ PM

HOURS DUE TO BAD WEATHER

ISSUED AND DELAYS

NOTE: ____

COMPLETION DATE	DAYS AHEAD OF SCHEDULE	DAYS BEHIND SCHEDULE

SAFETY AND INCIDENTS

SAFETY ISSUES THAT NEED TO BE ADDRESSED	ACCIDENTS / INCIDENTS / STEPS NEEDED TO RESOLVE

SUMMARY OF THE WORK DONE TODAY

IMPORTANT NOTES

NAME	SIGNATURE

TODAY LABOR

INITIALS	TRADE	START	FINISH	PAID HOURS	OVERTIME	COMPANY
☐ EMPLOYEE ☐ CONTRUCTOR		AM	PM			
☐ EMPLOYEE ☐ CONTRUCTOR		AM	PM			
☐ EMPLOYEE ☐ CONTRUCTOR		AM	PM			
☐ EMPLOYEE ☐ CONTRUCTOR		AM	PM			
☐ EMPLOYEE ☐ CONTRUCTOR		AM	PM			
☐ EMPLOYEE ☐ CONTRUCTOR		AM	PM			
☐ EMPLOYEE ☐ CONTRUCTOR		AM	PM			
☐ EMPLOYEE ☐ CONTRUCTOR		AM	PM			

EQUIPMENT ON SITE	NO. OF UNITE	WORKING YES / NO

HIRED EQUIPMENT	NO. OF UNITE	EQUIPMENT RENTED	FROM	RATE

NAME: ___________________________   SIGNATURE: ___________________________

MO TU WE TH FR SA SU
☐   ☐   ☐   ☐   ☐   ☐   ☐

DATE: /   /

PROJECT:

FOREMAN:

WEATHER

F°_____ C°_____   _____ AM _____ PM

HOURS DUE TO BAD WEATHER

ISSUED AND DELAYS

NOTE: ____

COMPLETION DATE	DAYS AHEAD OF SCHEDULE	DAYS BEHIND SCHEDULE

SAFETY AND INCIDENTS

SAFETY ISSUES THAT NEED TO BE ADDRESSED	ACCIDENTS / INCIDENTS / STEPS NEEDED TO RESOLVE

SUMMARY OF THE WORK DONE TODAY

IMPORTANT NOTES

NAME	SIGNATURE

TODAY LABOR

INITIALS	TRADE	START	FINISH	PAID HOURS	OVERTIME	COMPANY
☐ EMPLOYEE ☐ CONTRUCTOR		AM	PM			
☐ EMPLOYEE ☐ CONTRUCTOR		AM	PM			
☐ EMPLOYEE ☐ CONTRUCTOR		AM	PM			
☐ EMPLOYEE ☐ CONTRUCTOR		AM	PM			
☐ EMPLOYEE ☐ CONTRUCTOR		AM	PM			
☐ EMPLOYEE ☐ CONTRUCTOR		AM	PM			
☐ EMPLOYEE ☐ CONTRUCTOR		AM	PM			
☐ EMPLOYEE ☐ CONTRUCTOR		AM	PM			

EQUIPMENT ON SITE	NO. OF UNITE	WORKING YES / NO

HIRED EQUIPMENT	NO. OF UNITE	EQUIPMENT RENTED	FROM	RATE

NAME: _______________________   SIGNATURE: _______________________

MO TU WE TH FR SA SU

☐ ☐ ☐ ☐ ☐ ☐ ☐

DATE: / /

PROJECT:

FOREMAN:

WEATHER

F°_____ C°_____   _____ AM   _____ PM

HOURS DUE TO BAD WEATHER

ISSUED AND DELAYS

NOTE: ______________________

COMPLETION DATE	DAYS AHEAD OF SCHEDULE	DAYS BEHIND SCHEDULE

SAFETY AND INCIDENTS

SAFETY ISSUES THAT NEED TO BE ADDRESSED	ACCIDENTS / INCIDENTS / STEPS NEEDED TO RESOLVE

SUMMARY OF THE WORK DONE TODAY

IMPORTANT NOTES

NAME	SIGNATURE

TODAY LABOR

INITIALS	TRADE	START	FINISH	PAID HOURS	OVERTIME	COMPANY
☐ EMPLOYEE ☐ CONTRUCTOR		AM	PM			
☐ EMPLOYEE ☐ CONTRUCTOR		AM	PM			
☐ EMPLOYEE ☐ CONTRUCTOR		AM	PM			
☐ EMPLOYEE ☐ CONTRUCTOR		AM	PM			
☐ EMPLOYEE ☐ CONTRUCTOR		AM	PM			
☐ EMPLOYEE ☐ CONTRUCTOR		AM	PM			
☐ EMPLOYEE ☐ CONTRUCTOR		AM	PM			
☐ EMPLOYEE ☐ CONTRUCTOR		AM	PM			

EQUIPMENT ON SITE	NO. OF UNITE	WORKING YES / NO

HIRED EQUIPMENT	NO. OF UNITE	EQUIPMENT RENTED	FROM	RATE

NAME: _______________________   SIGNATURE: _______________________

MO TU WE TH FR SA SU
☐   ☐   ☐   ☐   ☐   ☐   ☐

DATE: /   /

PROJECT:

FOREMAN:

WEATHER   F°____ C°____   ____ AM ____ PM

HOURS DUE TO BAD WEATHER

ISSUED AND DELAYS

NOTE: ___________________________________

COMPLETION DATE	DAYS AHEAD OF SCHEDULE	DAYS BEHIND SCHEDULE

SAFETY AND INCIDENTS

SAFETY ISSUES THAT NEED TO BE ADDRESSED	ACCIDENTS / INCIDENTS / STEPS NEEDED TO RESOLVE

SUMMARY OF THE WORK DONE TODAY

IMPORTANT NOTES

NAME	SIGNATURE

TODAY LABOR

INITIALS	TRADE	START	FINISH	PAID HOURS	OVERTIME	COMPANY
☐ EMPLOYEE ☐ CONTRUCTOR		AM	PM			
☐ EMPLOYEE ☐ CONTRUCTOR		AM	PM			
☐ EMPLOYEE ☐ CONTRUCTOR		AM	PM			
☐ EMPLOYEE ☐ CONTRUCTOR		AM	PM			
☐ EMPLOYEE ☐ CONTRUCTOR		AM	PM			
☐ EMPLOYEE ☐ CONTRUCTOR		AM	PM			
☐ EMPLOYEE ☐ CONTRUCTOR		AM	PM			
☐ EMPLOYEE ☐ CONTRUCTOR		AM	PM			

EQUIPMENT ON SITE	NO. OF UNITE	WORKING YES / NO

HIRED EQUIPMENT	NO. OF UNITE	EQUIPMENT RENTED	FROM	RATE

NAME: _______________________   SIGNATURE: _______________________

MO TU WE TH FR SA SU
☐   ☐   ☐   ☐   ☐   ☐   ☐

DATE: ___ / ___ / ___

PROJECT:

FOREMAN:

WEATHER

F° ____ C° ____   ____ AM   ____ PM

HOURS DUE TO BAD WEATHER

ISSUED AND DELAYS

NOTE: ____

COMPLETION DATE	DAYS AHEAD OF SCHEDULE	DAYS BEHIND SCHEDULE

SAFETY AND INCIDENTS

SAFETY ISSUES THAT NEED TO BE ADDRESSED	ACCIDENTS / INCIDENTS / STEPS NEEDED TO RESOLVE

SUMMARY OF THE WORK DONE TODAY

IMPORTANT NOTES

NAME	SIGNATURE

TODAY LABOR

INITIALS	TRADE	START	FINISH	PAID HOURS	OVERTIME	COMPANY
☐ EMPLOYEE ☐ CONTRUCTOR		AM	PM			
☐ EMPLOYEE ☐ CONTRUCTOR		AM	PM			
☐ EMPLOYEE ☐ CONTRUCTOR		AM	PM			
☐ EMPLOYEE ☐ CONTRUCTOR		AM	PM			
☐ EMPLOYEE ☐ CONTRUCTOR		AM	PM			
☐ EMPLOYEE ☐ CONTRUCTOR		AM	PM			
☐ EMPLOYEE ☐ CONTRUCTOR		AM	PM			
☐ EMPLOYEE ☐ CONTRUCTOR		AM	PM			

EQUIPMENT ON SITE	NO. OF UNITE	WORKING YES / NO

HIRED EQUIPMENT	NO. OF UNITE	EQUIPMENT RENTED	FROM	RATE

NAME: _______________________________   SIGNATURE: _______________________________

MO   TU   WE   TH   FR   SA   SU
☐   ☐   ☐   ☐   ☐   ☐   ☐

DATE: /   /

PROJECT:

FOREMAN:

WEATHER

F° _____   C° _____   _____ AM   _____ PM

HOURS DUE TO
BAD WEATHER

ISSUED AND DELAYS

NOTE: ____

COMPLETION DATE	DAYS AHEAD OF SCHEDULE	DAYS BEHIND SCHEDULE

SAFETY AND INCIDENTS

SAFETY ISSUES THAT NEED TO BE ADDRESSED	ACCIDENTS / INCIDENTS / STEPS NEEDED TO RESOLVE

SUMMARY OF THE WORK DONE TODAY

IMPORTANT NOTES

NAME	SIGNATURE

TODAY LABOR

INITIALS	TRADE	START	FINISH	PAID HOURS	OVERTIME	COMPANY
☐ EMPLOYEE ☐ CONTRUCTOR		AM	PM			
☐ EMPLOYEE ☐ CONTRUCTOR		AM	PM			
☐ EMPLOYEE ☐ CONTRUCTOR		AM	PM			
☐ EMPLOYEE ☐ CONTRUCTOR		AM	PM			
☐ EMPLOYEE ☐ CONTRUCTOR		AM	PM			
☐ EMPLOYEE ☐ CONTRUCTOR		AM	PM			
☐ EMPLOYEE ☐ CONTRUCTOR		AM	PM			
☐ EMPLOYEE ☐ CONTRUCTOR		AM	PM			

EQUIPMENT ON SITE	NO. OF UNITE	WORKING YES / NO

HIRED EQUIPMENT	NO. OF UNITE	EQUIPMENT RENTED	FROM	RATE

NAME: _________________________   SIGNATURE: _________________________

MO   TU   WE   TH   FR   SA   SU
☐   ☐   ☐   ☐   ☐   ☐   ☐

DATE: __ / __ / __

PROJECT:

FOREMAN:

WEATHER

F° ____   C° ____   ____ AM   ____ PM

HOURS DUE TO BAD WEATHER	ISSUED AND DELAYS

NOTE: ______________________________________

COMPLETION DATE	DAYS AHEAD OF SCHEDULE	DAYS BEHIND SCHEDULE

SAFETY AND INCIDENTS

SAFETY ISSUES THAT NEED TO BE ADDRESSED	ACCIDENTS / INCIDENTS / STEPS NEEDED TO RESOLVE

SUMMARY OF THE WORK DONE TODAY

____
____
____
____
____

IMPORTANT NOTES

____
____
____
____
____

NAME	SIGNATURE

TODAY LABOR

INITIALS	TRADE	START	FINISH	PAID HOURS	OVERTIME	COMPANY
☐ EMPLOYEE ☐ CONTRUCTOR		AM	PM			
☐ EMPLOYEE ☐ CONTRUCTOR		AM	PM			
☐ EMPLOYEE ☐ CONTRUCTOR		AM	PM			
☐ EMPLOYEE ☐ CONTRUCTOR		AM	PM			
☐ EMPLOYEE ☐ CONTRUCTOR		AM	PM			
☐ EMPLOYEE ☐ CONTRUCTOR		AM	PM			
☐ EMPLOYEE ☐ CONTRUCTOR		AM	PM			
☐ EMPLOYEE ☐ CONTRUCTOR		AM	PM			

EQUIPMENT ON SITE	NO. OF UNITE	WORKING YES / NO

HIRED EQUIPMENT	NO. OF UNITE	EQUIPMENT RENTED	FROM	RATE

NAME: _______________________ SIGNATURE: _______________________

MO   TU   WE   TH   FR   SA   SU
☐   ☐   ☐   ☐   ☐   ☐   ☐

DATE: ____ / ____ / ____

PROJECT:

FOREMAN:

WEATHER

F°_____ C°_____   _____ AM _____ PM

HOURS DUE TO BAD WEATHER	ISSUED AND DELAYS

NOTE: ____

COMPLETION DATE	DAYS AHEAD OF SCHEDULE	DAYS BEHIND SCHEDULE

SAFETY AND INCIDENTS

SAFETY ISSUES THAT NEED TO BE ADDRESSED	ACCIDENTS / INCIDENTS / STEPS NEEDED TO RESOLVE

SUMMARY OF THE WORK DONE TODAY

IMPORTANT NOTES

NAME	SIGNATURE

TODAY LABOR

INITIALS	TRADE	START	FINISH	PAID HOURS	OVERTIME	COMPANY
☐ EMPLOYEE ☐ CONTRUCTOR		AM	PM			
☐ EMPLOYEE ☐ CONTRUCTOR		AM	PM			
☐ EMPLOYEE ☐ CONTRUCTOR		AM	PM			
☐ EMPLOYEE ☐ CONTRUCTOR		AM	PM			
☐ EMPLOYEE ☐ CONTRUCTOR		AM	PM			
☐ EMPLOYEE ☐ CONTRUCTOR		AM	PM			
☐ EMPLOYEE ☐ CONTRUCTOR		AM	PM			
☐ EMPLOYEE ☐ CONTRUCTOR		AM	PM			

EQUIPMENT ON SITE	NO. OF UNITE	WORKING YES / NO

HIRED EQUIPMENT	NO. OF UNITE	EQUIPMENT RENTED	FROM	RATE

NAME: _______________________   SIGNATURE: _______________________

MO TU WE TH FR SA SU
☐   ☐   ☐   ☐   ☐   ☐   ☐

DATE: ___ / ___ / ___

PROJECT:

FOREMAN:

WEATHER   F°_____ C°_____   _____ AM   _____ PM

HOURS DUE TO BAD WEATHER

ISSUED AND DELAYS

NOTE: ______________________________________

COMPLETION DATE	DAYS AHEAD OF SCHEDULE	DAYS BEHIND SCHEDULE

SAFETY AND INCIDENTS

SAFETY ISSUES THAT NEED TO BE ADDRESSED	ACCIDENTS / INCIDENTS / STEPS NEEDED TO RESOLVE

SUMMARY OF THE WORK DONE TODAY

IMPORTANT NOTES

NAME	SIGNATURE

TODAY LABOR

INITIALS	TRADE	START	FINISH	PAID HOURS	OVERTIME	COMPANY
☐ EMPLOYEE ☐ CONTRUCTOR		AM	PM			
☐ EMPLOYEE ☐ CONTRUCTOR		AM	PM			
☐ EMPLOYEE ☐ CONTRUCTOR		AM	PM			
☐ EMPLOYEE ☐ CONTRUCTOR		AM	PM			
☐ EMPLOYEE ☐ CONTRUCTOR		AM	PM			
☐ EMPLOYEE ☐ CONTRUCTOR		AM	PM			
☐ EMPLOYEE ☐ CONTRUCTOR		AM	PM			
☐ EMPLOYEE ☐ CONTRUCTOR		AM	PM			

EQUIPMENT ON SITE	NO. OF UNITE	WORKING YES / NO

HIRED EQUIPMENT	NO. OF UNITE	EQUIPMENT RENTED	FROM	RATE

NAME: _______________________ SIGNATURE: _______________________

MO TU WE TH FR SA SU

DATE: ___/___/___

PROJECT:

FOREMAN:

WEATHER

F°____ C°____ ____ AM ____ PM

HOURS DUE TO BAD WEATHER

ISSUED AND DELAYS

NOTE: ___________________________

COMPLETION DATE	DAYS AHEAD OF SCHEDULE	DAYS BEHIND SCHEDULE

SAFETY AND INCIDENTS

SAFETY ISSUES THAT NEED TO BE ADDRESSED	ACCIDENTS / INCIDENTS / STEPS NEEDED TO RESOLVE

SUMMARY OF THE WORK DONE TODAY

IMPORTANT NOTES

NAME	SIGNATURE

TODAY LABOR

INITIALS	TRADE	START	FINISH	PAID HOURS	OVERTIME	COMPANY
☐ EMPLOYEE ☐ CONTRUCTOR		AM	PM			
☐ EMPLOYEE ☐ CONTRUCTOR		AM	PM			
☐ EMPLOYEE ☐ CONTRUCTOR		AM	PM			
☐ EMPLOYEE ☐ CONTRUCTOR		AM	PM			
☐ EMPLOYEE ☐ CONTRUCTOR		AM	PM			
☐ EMPLOYEE ☐ CONTRUCTOR		AM	PM			
☐ EMPLOYEE ☐ CONTRUCTOR		AM	PM			
☐ EMPLOYEE ☐ CONTRUCTOR		AM	PM			

EQUIPMENT ON SITE	NO. OF UNITE	WORKING YES / NO

HIRED EQUIPMENT	NO. OF UNITE	EQUIPMENT RENTED	FROM	RATE

NAME: _______________________   SIGNATURE: _______________________

MO   TU   WE   TH   FR   SA   SU
☐   ☐   ☐   ☐   ☐   ☐   ☐

DATE: /   /

PROJECT:

FOREMAN:

WEATHER

F°_____   C°_____   _____ AM   _____ PM

| HOURS DUE TO BAD WEATHER | ISSUED AND DELAYS |

NOTE: ____

COMPLETION DATE	DAYS AHEAD OF SCHEDULE	DAYS BEHIND SCHEDULE

SAFETY AND INCIDENTS

SAFETY ISSUES THAT NEED TO BE ADDRESSED	ACCIDENTS / INCIDENTS / STEPS NEEDED TO RESOLVE

SUMMARY OF THE WORK DONE TODAY

IMPORTANT NOTES

NAME	SIGNATURE

TODAY LABOR

INITIALS	TRADE	START	FINISH	PAID HOURS	OVERTIME	COMPANY
☐ EMPLOYEE ☐ CONTRUCTOR		AM	PM			
☐ EMPLOYEE ☐ CONTRUCTOR		AM	PM			
☐ EMPLOYEE ☐ CONTRUCTOR		AM	PM			
☐ EMPLOYEE ☐ CONTRUCTOR		AM	PM			
☐ EMPLOYEE ☐ CONTRUCTOR		AM	PM			
☐ EMPLOYEE ☐ CONTRUCTOR		AM	PM			
☐ EMPLOYEE ☐ CONTRUCTOR		AM	PM			
☐ EMPLOYEE ☐ CONTRUCTOR		AM	PM			

EQUIPMENT ON SITE	NO. OF UNITE	WORKING YES / NO

HIRED EQUIPMENT	NO. OF UNITE	EQUIPMENT RENTED	FROM	RATE

NAME: ______________________________   SIGNATURE: ______________________________

MO   TU   WE   TH   FR   SA   SU
☐   ☐   ☐   ☐   ☐   ☐   ☐

DATE: ___/___/___

PROJECT:

FOREMAN:

WEATHER

F°_____ C°_____   _____AM   _____PM

HOURS DUE TO BAD WEATHER

ISSUED AND DELAYS

NOTE: _______________________________________

COMPLETION DATE	DAYS AHEAD OF SCHEDULE	DAYS BEHIND SCHEDULE

SAFETY AND INCIDENTS

SAFETY ISSUES THAT NEED TO BE ADDRESSED	ACCIDENTS / INCIDENTS / STEPS NEEDED TO RESOLVE

SUMMARY OF THE WORK DONE TODAY

IMPORTANT NOTES

NAME	SIGNATURE

TODAY LABOR

INITIALS	TRADE	START	FINISH	PAID HOURS	OVERTIME	COMPANY
☐ EMPLOYEE ☐ CONTRUCTOR		AM	PM			
☐ EMPLOYEE ☐ CONTRUCTOR		AM	PM			
☐ EMPLOYEE ☐ CONTRUCTOR		AM	PM			
☐ EMPLOYEE ☐ CONTRUCTOR		AM	PM			
☐ EMPLOYEE ☐ CONTRUCTOR		AM	PM			
☐ EMPLOYEE ☐ CONTRUCTOR		AM	PM			
☐ EMPLOYEE ☐ CONTRUCTOR		AM	PM			
☐ EMPLOYEE ☐ CONTRUCTOR		AM	PM			

EQUIPMENT ON SITE	NO. OF UNITE	WORKING YES / NO

HIRED EQUIPMENT	NO. OF UNITE	EQUIPMENT RENTED	FROM	RATE

NAME: _______________________   SIGNATURE: _______________________

MO TU WE TH FR SA SU
☐   ☐   ☐   ☐   ☐   ☐   ☐

DATE: ___ / ___ / ___

PROJECT:

FOREMAN:

WEATHER

F°____ C°____ ____AM ____PM

HOURS DUE TO BAD WEATHER

ISSUED AND DELAYS

NOTE: ____

COMPLETION DATE	DAYS AHEAD OF SCHEDULE	DAYS BEHIND SCHEDULE

SAFETY AND INCIDENTS

SAFETY ISSUES THAT NEED TO BE ADDRESSED	ACCIDENTS / INCIDENTS / STEPS NEEDED TO RESOLVE

SUMMARY OF THE WORK DONE TODAY

IMPORTANT NOTES

NAME	SIGNATURE

TODAY LABOR

INITIALS	TRADE	START	FINISH	PAID HOURS	OVERTIME	COMPANY
☐ EMPLOYEE ☐ CONTRUCTOR		AM	PM			
☐ EMPLOYEE ☐ CONTRUCTOR		AM	PM			
☐ EMPLOYEE ☐ CONTRUCTOR		AM	PM			
☐ EMPLOYEE ☐ CONTRUCTOR		AM	PM			
☐ EMPLOYEE ☐ CONTRUCTOR		AM	PM			
☐ EMPLOYEE ☐ CONTRUCTOR		AM	PM			
☐ EMPLOYEE ☐ CONTRUCTOR		AM	PM			
☐ EMPLOYEE ☐ CONTRUCTOR		AM	PM			

EQUIPMENT ON SITE	NO. OF UNITE	WORKING YES / NO

HIRED EQUIPMENT	NO. OF UNITE	EQUIPMENT RENTED	FROM	RATE

NAME: _______________________   SIGNATURE: _______________________

MO TU WE TH FR SA SU
☐   ☐   ☐   ☐   ☐   ☐   ☐

DATE: /   /

PROJECT:

FOREMAN:

WEATHER   F°_____ C°_____   _____ AM   _____ PM

HOURS DUE TO BAD WEATHER

ISSUED AND DELAYS

NOTE: ____________________

COMPLETION DATE	DAYS AHEAD OF SCHEDULE	DAYS BEHIND SCHEDULE

SAFETY AND INCIDENTS

SAFETY ISSUES THAT NEED TO BE ADDRESSED	ACCIDENTS / INCIDENTS / STEPS NEEDED TO RESOLVE

SUMMARY OF THE WORK DONE TODAY

IMPORTANT NOTES

NAME	SIGNATURE

TODAY LABOR

INITIALS	TRADE	START	FINISH	PAID HOURS	OVERTIME	COMPANY
☐ EMPLOYEE ☐ CONTRUCTOR		AM	PM			
☐ EMPLOYEE ☐ CONTRUCTOR		AM	PM			
☐ EMPLOYEE ☐ CONTRUCTOR		AM	PM			
☐ EMPLOYEE ☐ CONTRUCTOR		AM	PM			
☐ EMPLOYEE ☐ CONTRUCTOR		AM	PM			
☐ EMPLOYEE ☐ CONTRUCTOR		AM	PM			
☐ EMPLOYEE ☐ CONTRUCTOR		AM	PM			
☐ EMPLOYEE ☐ CONTRUCTOR		AM	PM			

EQUIPMENT ON SITE	NO. OF UNITE	WORKING YES / NO

HIRED EQUIPMENT	NO. OF UNITE	EQUIPMENT RENTED	FROM	RATE

NAME: ___________________________   SIGNATURE: ___________________________

MO TU WE TH FR SA SU
☐   ☐   ☐   ☐   ☐   ☐   ☐

DATE: ___ / ___ / ___

PROJECT:

FOREMAN:

WEATHER

F° ____ C° ____   ____ AM ____ PM

HOURS DUE TO BAD WEATHER

ISSUED AND DELAYS

NOTE: ____

COMPLETION DATE	DAYS AHEAD OF SCHEDULE	DAYS BEHIND SCHEDULE

SAFETY AND INCIDENTS

SAFETY ISSUES THAT NEED TO BE ADDRESSED	ACCIDENTS / INCIDENTS / STEPS NEEDED TO RESOLVE

SUMMARY OF THE WORK DONE TODAY

IMPORTANT NOTES

NAME	SIGNATURE

TODAY LABOR

INITIALS	TRADE	START	FINISH	PAID HOURS	OVERTIME	COMPANY
☐ EMPLOYEE ☐ CONTRUCTOR		AM	PM			
☐ EMPLOYEE ☐ CONTRUCTOR		AM	PM			
☐ EMPLOYEE ☐ CONTRUCTOR		AM	PM			
☐ EMPLOYEE ☐ CONTRUCTOR		AM	PM			
☐ EMPLOYEE ☐ CONTRUCTOR		AM	PM			
☐ EMPLOYEE ☐ CONTRUCTOR		AM	PM			
☐ EMPLOYEE ☐ CONTRUCTOR		AM	PM			
☐ EMPLOYEE ☐ CONTRUCTOR		AM	PM			

EQUIPMENT ON SITE	NO. OF UNITE	WORKING YES / NO

HIRED EQUIPMENT	NO. OF UNITE	EQUIPMENT RENTED	FROM	RATE

NAME: ______________________   SIGNATURE: ______________________

MO TU WE TH FR SA SU
☐   ☐   ☐   ☐   ☐   ☐   ☐

DATE: ___ / ___ / ___

PROJECT: _______________

FOREMAN: _______________

WEATHER

F° ___ C° ___   _____ AM _____ PM

HOURS DUE TO BAD WEATHER

ISSUED AND DELAYS

NOTE: _______________

COMPLETION DATE	DAYS AHEAD OF SCHEDULE	DAYS BEHIND SCHEDULE

SAFETY AND INCIDENTS

SAFETY ISSUES THAT NEED TO BE ADDRESSED	ACCIDENTS / INCIDENTS / STEPS NEEDED TO RESOLVE

SUMMARY OF THE WORK DONE TODAY

IMPORTANT NOTES

NAME	SIGNATURE

TODAY LABOR

INITIALS	TRADE	START	FINISH	PAID HOURS	OVERTIME	COMPANY
☐ EMPLOYEE ☐ CONTRUCTOR		AM	PM			
☐ EMPLOYEE ☐ CONTRUCTOR		AM	PM			
☐ EMPLOYEE ☐ CONTRUCTOR		AM	PM			
☐ EMPLOYEE ☐ CONTRUCTOR		AM	PM			
☐ EMPLOYEE ☐ CONTRUCTOR		AM	PM			
☐ EMPLOYEE ☐ CONTRUCTOR		AM	PM			
☐ EMPLOYEE ☐ CONTRUCTOR		AM	PM			
☐ EMPLOYEE ☐ CONTRUCTOR		AM	PM			

EQUIPMENT ON SITE	NO. OF UNITE	WORKING YES / NO

HIRED EQUIPMENT	NO. OF UNITE	EQUIPMENT RENTED	FROM	RATE

NAME: _______________________   SIGNATURE: _______________________

MO   TU   WE   TH   FR   SA   SU
☐   ☐   ☐   ☐   ☐   ☐   ☐

DATE: ___ / ___ / ___

PROJECT:

FOREMAN:

WEATHER
F° _____ C° _____   _____ AM   _____ PM

| HOURS DUE TO BAD WEATHER | ISSUED AND DELAYS |

NOTE: _______________________________

COMPLETION DATE	DAYS AHEAD OF SCHEDULE	DAYS BEHIND SCHEDULE

SAFETY AND INCIDENTS

SAFETY ISSUES THAT NEED TO BE ADDRESSED	ACCIDENTS / INCIDENTS / STEPS NEEDED TO RESOLVE

SUMMARY OF THE WORK DONE TODAY

IMPORTANT NOTES

NAME	SIGNATURE

TODAY LABOR

INITIALS	TRADE	START	FINISH	PAID HOURS	OVERTIME	COMPANY
☐ EMPLOYEE ☐ CONTRUCTOR		AM	PM			
☐ EMPLOYEE ☐ CONTRUCTOR		AM	PM			
☐ EMPLOYEE ☐ CONTRUCTOR		AM	PM			
☐ EMPLOYEE ☐ CONTRUCTOR		AM	PM			
☐ EMPLOYEE ☐ CONTRUCTOR		AM	PM			
☐ EMPLOYEE ☐ CONTRUCTOR		AM	PM			
☐ EMPLOYEE ☐ CONTRUCTOR		AM	PM			
☐ EMPLOYEE ☐ CONTRUCTOR		AM	PM			

EQUIPMENT ON SITE	NO. OF UNITE	WORKING YES / NO

HIRED EQUIPMENT	NO. OF UNITE	EQUIPMENT RENTED	FROM	RATE

NAME: ______________________________   SIGNATURE: ______________________________

MO TU WE TH FR SA SU
☐   ☐   ☐   ☐   ☐   ☐   ☐

DATE: __/__/__

PROJECT:

FOREMAN:

WEATHER

F°____ C°____ ____ AM ____ PM

HOURS DUE TO BAD WEATHER

ISSUED AND DELAYS

NOTE: _______________________________

COMPLETION DATE	DAYS AHEAD OF SCHEDULE	DAYS BEHIND SCHEDULE

SAFETY AND INCIDENTS

SAFETY ISSUES THAT NEED TO BE ADDRESSED	ACCIDENTS / INCIDENTS / STEPS NEEDED TO RESOLVE

SUMMARY OF THE WORK DONE TODAY

IMPORTANT NOTES

NAME	SIGNATURE

TODAY LABOR

INITIALS	TRADE	START	FINISH	PAID HOURS	OVERTIME	COMPANY
☐ EMPLOYEE ☐ CONTRUCTOR		AM	PM			
☐ EMPLOYEE ☐ CONTRUCTOR		AM	PM			
☐ EMPLOYEE ☐ CONTRUCTOR		AM	PM			
☐ EMPLOYEE ☐ CONTRUCTOR		AM	PM			
☐ EMPLOYEE ☐ CONTRUCTOR		AM	PM			
☐ EMPLOYEE ☐ CONTRUCTOR		AM	PM			
☐ EMPLOYEE ☐ CONTRUCTOR		AM	PM			
☐ EMPLOYEE ☐ CONTRUCTOR		AM	PM			

EQUIPMENT ON SITE	NO. OF UNITE	WORKING YES / NO

HIRED EQUIPMENT	NO. OF UNITE	EQUIPMENT RENTED	FROM	RATE

NAME: _______________________________   SIGNATURE: _______________________________

MO TU WE TH FR SA SU

DATE: ___/___/___

PROJECT:

FOREMAN:

WEATHER

F°_____ C°_____ _____AM _____PM

| HOURS DUE TO BAD WEATHER | ISSUED AND DELAYS |

NOTE: ____

| COMPLETION DATE | DAYS AHEAD OF SCHEDULE | DAYS BEHIND SCHEDULE |

SAFETY AND INCIDENTS

| SAFETY ISSUES THAT NEED TO BE ADDRESSED | ACCIDENTS / INCIDENTS / STEPS NEEDED TO RESOLVE |

SUMMARY OF THE WORK DONE TODAY

IMPORTANT NOTES

| NAME | SIGNATURE |

TODAY LABOR

INITIALS	TRADE	START	FINISH	PAID HOURS	OVERTIME	COMPANY
☐ EMPLOYEE ☐ CONTRUCTOR		AM	PM			
☐ EMPLOYEE ☐ CONTRUCTOR		AM	PM			
☐ EMPLOYEE ☐ CONTRUCTOR		AM	PM			
☐ EMPLOYEE ☐ CONTRUCTOR		AM	PM			
☐ EMPLOYEE ☐ CONTRUCTOR		AM	PM			
☐ EMPLOYEE ☐ CONTRUCTOR		AM	PM			
☐ EMPLOYEE ☐ CONTRUCTOR		AM	PM			
☐ EMPLOYEE ☐ CONTRUCTOR		AM	PM			

EQUIPMENT ON SITE	NO. OF UNITE	WORKING YES / NO

HIRED EQUIPMENT	NO. OF UNITE	EQUIPMENT RENTED	FROM	RATE

NAME: _______________________   SIGNATURE: _______________________

MO   TU   WE   TH   FR   SA   SU
☐   ☐   ☐   ☐   ☐   ☐   ☐

DATE: ___/___/___

PROJECT:

FOREMAN:

WEATHER   F°____ C°____   ____ AM   ____ PM

HOURS DUE TO BAD WEATHER	ISSUED AND DELAYS

NOTE: ____

COMPLETION DATE	DAYS AHEAD OF SCHEDULE	DAYS BEHIND SCHEDULE

SAFETY AND INCIDENTS

SAFETY ISSUES THAT NEED TO BE ADDRESSED	ACCIDENTS / INCIDENTS / STEPS NEEDED TO RESOLVE

SUMMARY OF THE WORK DONE TODAY

IMPORTANT NOTES

NAME	SIGNATURE

TODAY LABOR

INITIALS	TRADE	START	FINISH	PAID HOURS	OVERTIME	COMPANY
☐ EMPLOYEE ☐ CONTRUCTOR		AM	PM			
☐ EMPLOYEE ☐ CONTRUCTOR		AM	PM			
☐ EMPLOYEE ☐ CONTRUCTOR		AM	PM			
☐ EMPLOYEE ☐ CONTRUCTOR		AM	PM			
☐ EMPLOYEE ☐ CONTRUCTOR		AM	PM			
☐ EMPLOYEE ☐ CONTRUCTOR		AM	PM			
☐ EMPLOYEE ☐ CONTRUCTOR		AM	PM			
☐ EMPLOYEE ☐ CONTRUCTOR		AM	PM			

EQUIPMENT ON SITE	NO. OF UNITE	WORKING YES / NO

HIRED EQUIPMENT	NO. OF UNITE	EQUIPMENT RENTED	FROM	RATE

NAME: ________________________   SIGNATURE: ________________________

MO TU WE TH FR SA SU

DATE: /   /

PROJECT:

FOREMAN:

WEATHER

F°____ C°____   ____AM ____PM

| HOURS DUE TO BAD WEATHER | ISSUED AND DELAYS |

NOTE: ____________________________

| COMPLETION DATE | DAYS AHEAD OF SCHEDULE | DAYS BEHIND SCHEDULE |

SAFETY AND INCIDENTS

| SAFETY ISSUES THAT NEED TO BE ADDRESSED | ACCIDENTS / INCIDENTS / STEPS NEEDED TO RESOLVE |

SUMMARY OF THE WORK DONE TODAY

IMPORTANT NOTES

| NAME | SIGNATURE |

TODAY LABOR

INITIALS	TRADE	START	FINISH	PAID HOURS	OVERTIME	COMPANY
☐ EMPLOYEE ☐ CONTRUCTOR		AM	PM			
☐ EMPLOYEE ☐ CONTRUCTOR		AM	PM			
☐ EMPLOYEE ☐ CONTRUCTOR		AM	PM			
☐ EMPLOYEE ☐ CONTRUCTOR		AM	PM			
☐ EMPLOYEE ☐ CONTRUCTOR		AM	PM			
☐ EMPLOYEE ☐ CONTRUCTOR		AM	PM			
☐ EMPLOYEE ☐ CONTRUCTOR		AM	PM			
☐ EMPLOYEE ☐ CONTRUCTOR		AM	PM			

EQUIPMENT ON SITE	NO. OF UNITE	WORKING YES / NO

HIRED EQUIPMENT	NO. OF UNITE	EQUIPMENT RENTED	FROM	RATE

NAME: _______________________   SIGNATURE: _______________________

MO	TU	WE	TH	FR	SA	SU
☐	☐	☐	☐	☐	☐	☐

DATE: ___ / ___ / ___

PROJECT:

FOREMAN:

WEATHER

F° _____ C° _____   _____ AM _____ PM

HOURS DUE TO BAD WEATHER

ISSUED AND DELAYS

NOTE: _______________________________

COMPLETION DATE	DAYS AHEAD OF SCHEDULE	DAYS BEHIND SCHEDULE

SAFETY AND INCIDENTS

SAFETY ISSUES THAT NEED TO BE ADDRESSED	ACCIDENTS / INCIDENTS / STEPS NEEDED TO RESOLVE

SUMMARY OF THE WORK DONE TODAY

IMPORTANT NOTES

NAME	SIGNATURE

TODAY LABOR

INITIALS	TRADE	START	FINISH	PAID HOURS	OVERTIME	COMPANY
☐ EMPLOYEE ☐ CONTRUCTOR		AM	PM			
☐ EMPLOYEE ☐ CONTRUCTOR		AM	PM			
☐ EMPLOYEE ☐ CONTRUCTOR		AM	PM			
☐ EMPLOYEE ☐ CONTRUCTOR		AM	PM			
☐ EMPLOYEE ☐ CONTRUCTOR		AM	PM			
☐ EMPLOYEE ☐ CONTRUCTOR		AM	PM			
☐ EMPLOYEE ☐ CONTRUCTOR		AM	PM			
☐ EMPLOYEE ☐ CONTRUCTOR		AM	PM			

EQUIPMENT ON SITE	NO. OF UNITE	WORKING YES / NO

HIRED EQUIPMENT	NO. OF UNITE	EQUIPMENT RENTED	FROM	RATE

NAME: _______________________   SIGNATURE: _______________________

MO TU WE TH FR SA SU
☐   ☐   ☐   ☐   ☐   ☐   ☐

DATE: /   /

PROJECT:

FOREMAN:

WEATHER

F°_____ C°_____   _____ AM _____ PM

HOURS DUE TO BAD WEATHER

ISSUED AND DELAYS

NOTE: ____

COMPLETION DATE	DAYS AHEAD OF SCHEDULE	DAYS BEHIND SCHEDULE

SAFETY AND INCIDENTS

SAFETY ISSUES THAT NEED TO BE ADDRESSED	ACCIDENTS / INCIDENTS / STEPS NEEDED TO RESOLVE

SUMMARY OF THE WORK DONE TODAY

IMPORTANT NOTES

NAME	SIGNATURE

TODAY LABOR

INITIALS	TRADE	START	FINISH	PAID HOURS	OVERTIME	COMPANY
☐ EMPLOYEE ☐ CONTRUCTOR		AM	PM			
☐ EMPLOYEE ☐ CONTRUCTOR		AM	PM			
☐ EMPLOYEE ☐ CONTRUCTOR		AM	PM			
☐ EMPLOYEE ☐ CONTRUCTOR		AM	PM			
☐ EMPLOYEE ☐ CONTRUCTOR		AM	PM			
☐ EMPLOYEE ☐ CONTRUCTOR		AM	PM			
☐ EMPLOYEE ☐ CONTRUCTOR		AM	PM			
☐ EMPLOYEE ☐ CONTRUCTOR		AM	PM			

EQUIPMENT ON SITE	NO. OF UNITE	WORKING YES / NO

HIRED EQUIPMENT	NO. OF UNITE	EQUIPMENT RENTED	FROM	RATE

NAME: _______________________   SIGNATURE: _______________________

IMPORTANT TELEPHONE NUMBER

▶ NAME _______________________________ PHONE _______________________________
   EMAIL ____

▶ NAME _______________________________ PHONE _______________________________
   EMAIL ____

▶ NAME _______________________________ PHONE _______________________________
   EMAIL ____

▶ NAME _______________________________ PHONE _______________________________
   EMAIL ____

▶ NAME _______________________________ PHONE _______________________________
   EMAIL ____

▶ NAME _______________________________ PHONE _______________________________
   EMAIL ____

▶ NAME _______________________________ PHONE _______________________________
   EMAIL ____

▶ NAME _______________________________ PHONE _______________________________
   EMAIL ____

▶ NAME _______________________________ PHONE _______________________________
   EMAIL ____

▶ NAME _______________________________ PHONE _______________________________
   EMAIL ____

▶ NAME _______________________________ PHONE _______________________________
   EMAIL ____

▶ NAME _______________________________ PHONE _______________________________
   EMAIL ____

▶ NAME _______________________________ PHONE _______________________________
   EMAIL ____